AF248548

the "Atheism" of the Early Church

Rousas John Rushdoony

ROSS HOUSE BOOKS

vallecito, california

Copyright 1983
Rousas John Rushdoony

1983 printing published by Logos Foundation

2000 printing published by

Ross House Books
PO BOX 67
Vallecito, California, USA
www.rosshousebooks.org

No part of this book may be
reproduced in any form without
permission in writing from the publisher.

Library of Congress Catalog Card Number: 00-090840
ISBN: 1-879998-18-1

Printed in the United States of America

Other books by
Rousas John Rushdoony

The Institutes of Biblical Law, Vol. I
The Institutes of Biblical Law, Vol. II, Law & Society
The Institutes of Biblical Law, Vol. III, The Intent of the Law
The Gospel of John
The Biblical Philosophy of History
Systematic Theology
Foundations of Social Order
Politics of Guilt and Pity
Christianity and the State
Salvation and Godly Rule
The Messianic Character of American Education
Roots of Reconstruction
The One and the Many
Revolt Against Maturity
By What Standard?
Law & Liberty

For a complete listing of available books by Rousas John Rushdoony
and other Christian reconstructionists, contact:

ROSS HOUSE BOOKS
PO Box 67
Vallecito, CA 95251
www.rosshousebooks.org

Table of Contents

Year 2000 Publication

Early in the 1980s, I made several trips to Australia. They were very successful, and, during one of the early ones, I gave a series of talks reproduced in this little book.

I believe these essays to be important because the church today is beginning to face a situation similar to that of the early church in the Roman Empire. Where the church is *truly* faithful to Scripture, it is seen as an enemy of the state, and with good reason. The Bible requires a lord other than the state, and a radically different kind of education and law. It is Christ who is our Lord, not the state.

The modern state is religious but anti-Christian. It claims lordship and rejects Christ as Lord. As a result, we are everywhere seeing the rise of a working atheism.

Christians cannot believe in the lordship or sovereignty of the state. Jesus Christ alone is Lord. We must reject all other claims to sovereignty. Step by step, the church has receded from the law of God and His sovereignty. It has become peripheral to society and has surrendered leadership to the state. Either we reverse this process, or the church is finished.

Rousas John Rushdoony
Vallecito, California
September 28, 2000

The Place of the Judeo-Christian Ethic in Today's Society

"ISSUE: Without order we will have anarchy. What kind of order? The 'Brave New World' of Aldous Huxley? A society controlled by the ferocious ideology of Orwell's garrison state? Or the order which arises out of the Christian ethic, as found in God's law-word, the Bible!

Since all education is religious, with the ultimate goal of remaking society, the options are secular Humanism or Christianity. A Christian school is essential.

That is where religious freedom and the God-directed responsibility of parents and churches must be defended at all costs. The State is not Lord, but Jesus Christ is Lord!"

Harold Carter

In May of 1983, Logos Foundation convened a two-day conference at the Shore Motor Inn in Artarmon, Sydney, which addressed the subject, "The Place of the Judeo-Christian Ethic in Today's Society." Speakers were Mr. William Bentley Ball and Professor Rousas J. Rushdoony. Mr. Ball approached the discussion from a legal standpoint; Dr. Rushdoony spoke from a theological view.

While both men are Americans, it soon became obvious that there is a striking parallel between America and Australia regarding the attack by the State upon Christian schools, with America several years ahead of Australia in responding to and countering challenges to Christ-centered education. In that regard, the experience of these men was most timely, as challenges continue to mount day-by-day against the very existence of Christian schools in Australia.

The timeliness, the value, and the depth of the meetings was such that all delegates considered it vital to have the audio recordings of the meetings transcribed and edited for publication. Dr. Rushdoony's six messages are the subject of this book.

Chapter One

The "Atheism" of the Early Church

Peter's message to the elders and scribes, recorded in Acts 4:12, best sums up the conflict we are involved in today:

> Neither is there salvation in any other; for there is none other name under heaven given among men, whereby we must be saved.

It is important for us to understand the context of this verse. With that statement, Peter effectually issued a spiritual declaration of war against the Roman Empire. When Augustus Caesar took the helm in Rome and had consolidated his power, a great celebration was held throughout the Roman Empire. It was called the "Advent" celebration — a very significant term, and a very religious one. It was the Advent celebration because Augustus Caesar had *come*, in all the fullness of his power. The heralds — again an interesting word — were sent to the far corners of the Roman Empire with a great Advent proclamation: "There is none other name under heaven whereby men may be saved than the name of Augustus Caesar!" It was the proclamation of Caesar, of the state, as man's savior.

We can understand, then, why conflict between Christ and the Caesars was inevitable, why the church went through all the troubles it did, year in and year out, and why men were martyred for the faith. It was because of this question: "Who is the Lord, or sovereign? Who is the savior?"

The modern state is saying again, as the Caesars did of old, "We are the lord. We are the sovereigns over creation." The words "sovereign" and "lord" are identical. They are different words for the same thing. We cannot confess the sovereignty of the state *and* the sovereignty of Christ. We must affirm, as the early church did, that Christ is Lord also over Caesar. Every man, every institution, every civil government, every school, all things, must in due time acknowledge the lordship or the sovereignty of Christ, for there is salvation in no other. "There is none other name under heaven given among men whereby we must be saved."

The "Atheism" of the Early Church is an unusual title, and I do not believe, of course, that the early church was atheistic. Rather, the Empire claimed that this new institution was an atheistic agency. It was also charged with serious offenses, in particular cannibalism and incest. Scholars have by and large neglected these charges. I do not know of a single one who has analyzed these charges by the Roman Empire against the early church. They are usually dismissed as evidence of the kind of slander to which Christians were subjected. But as we examine the literature of the early church and the church's reactions to these charges, as well as the actual charges themselves, we realize that we had better take Rome's allegations rather seriously and understand what they meant.

The interesting fact is that the charges came, not from the people in the street, but from the philosophers — men of prestige, men who, from our perspective, should have known better. This was the thing that upset and offended Christians. They were facing a most serious charge — and it came from the best in Rome, not the worst.

There was a conflict between Rome and the early church. Rome's policy towards all religions was that no religion had a right to exist unless it was a licit religion, duly licensed by the Empire, and possessing a certificate of validation which members of that religion or cult were required to display on the walls of their meeting-place. A part of the procedure whereby that licit status was secured was to appear before a Roman imperial center, and there to put a little incense on a brazier before an image of the emperor or a battle insignia, and then declare very briefly, "Caesar is Lord!" That was all. It was an acknowledgment of the sovereignty of Caesar over every area of life and thought.

But the Christians felt that they had been called instead to bring everything into captivity to Jesus Christ. We know from the research, for example, of J.N.D. Kelly, a British historian, that the baptismal confession, required of all believers in the early church, was to stand before the congregation and declare, "Jesus is Lord," or "Jesus Christ is Lord." In so doing Christians put their heads on the chopping-block. They became a subversive force because through their confession they denied the lordship of Caesar. This is what the conflict was about. Who was the Lord — Christ or Caesar?

The position of the early church was that Christ is Lord over Caesar, not Caesar over Christ. Christians refused to accept the status of a licit religion. This was the battle which was fought over and over again throughout the Middle Ages. There was a time when the church surrendered, and the results were very serious. It became the pawn of the aristocracy in Rome and the pawn of the Holy Roman emperors. But, especially with Hildebrand, the church began to assert again the Lordship of Christ. That same battle is very much with us again. Unless we recognize our roots in the Scripture, in the early church, and in the Middle Ages, we will fail to realize the wealth that is ours as Christians. Battles for which Christian saints died will be surrendered.

Rome hated atheism as a subversive force, and Christianity was charged with being an atheistic cult. Rome was very happy with religion in general, because religion ostensibly provided the social cement, the cohesive force that people needed to bind them one to another. This view of religion as a form of "social cement" was an entirely naturalistic one.

Rome carefully examined every new religion which came along. It received reports from officials on each one, as soon as they encountered it. We have recorded a letter from Pliny containing one such report — and there must have been a multitude of them going to Caesar — about this new religion which was beginning to spread throughout the Empire. And, of course, there was a demand that this new cult seek recognition as soon as possible. Up until the Jewish-Roman war of A.D. 66-70, a good deal of tolerance was accorded to this new movement, because it was seen as a part of Judaism. But with the Jewish-Roman War, that tolerance for anything associated with those troublesome people in Judea ended. There began an insistent demand that these groups seek licensure and that they submit to any and all controls. Thus began the martyrdoms and persecutions which extended over the generations until Constantine (a very much abused man, by the way) recognized Christianity.

But the attacks upon Christianity did not end with Constantine. His successors attempted to reintroduce paganism in the form of heresy, notably Arianism, and later Pelagianism. This, in effect, reintroduced paganism in a Christian guise, the goal still being the control of religion by the state.

Sometimes the Empire courted the church. At least one, possibly two, emperors had images of Jesus put into their private chapels, and the word was given out, "The emperor loves Jesus as much as you do. In fact, he has His image in the chapel and he sometimes prays to Him. Why are you opposed to the sovereignty of the emperor?" But such attempts failed. Meanwhile, the charge was very earnestly raised that the Christians were atheists and that they were no doubt involved in all kinds of fearful practices.

Two battles, which marked the early church from the beginning, we still have with us today. The first was over the question of sovereignty or lordship, and the second was over the issue of abortion. Abortion was entirely legal within the Empire, but the early church instituted very severe penalties against any of its members involved in this very common practice. But that is not all. At the same time, the early church began to deal with the results of this world of abortion.

Not every abortionist in those days functioned with the cold and brutal efficiency common to us now. Therefore, they were not always successful in aborting babies. As a result, when the unwanted babies were born, they were promptly taken and abandoned under the bridges of the river Tiber in Rome. In other cities there were places which were routinely used for abandoning babies.

The Christians made it their habit immediately to go to the places where these babies were abandoned — to be devoured, as Tertullian said, by wild dogs — to collect these infants and parcel them out from family to family. This tells us something about the life of faith among these believers. How many members of congregations today would welcome an officer of the church coming by with an abandoned baby or two, and feel it was their duty to rear them in faith!

Rome was very indignant about this practice, because it did not make her look at all good. As a matter of fact, Rome legislated against it at one period, but within a year it had to repeal the legislation, because it made the Empire look so bad officially. Moreover, since the births were not registered, the babies involved were nonexistent persons, and what law could you make regarding a practice involving nonexistent people! It was very difficult for the imperial lawyers to contend with such a practice, but it was not for lack of efforts!

Thus the charge was made that these babies were collected for cannibalism — for the communion feasts of the early church. This was one source of the accusation of cannibalism raised against the early church. Of course, there was very little evidence for it, and it was a charge that did not succeed. After all, it was obvious that these Christian families had many extra children of their own. All the same, the charges of incest and cannibalism persisted. Why? Because they were part and parcel of the charge of atheism. Moreover, the attitude of the logical-thinking Roman philosophers was, "We may not have evidence that they do these things, but logically it is necessary that they do them."

These charges were a major concern to the early church, and Justin Martyr said concerning them, "We confess that we are atheists so far as gods of this sort are concerned, but not with respect to the most true God, the Father of righteousness and temperance and the other virtues, who is free from all impurity."

Against the cynic philosopher Crescens, who accused the church of atheism, Justin Martyr, in his *Second Apology*, said, "I too therefore expect to be plotted against and fixed to the stake by some of those I have named, or perhaps by Crescens, that lover of bravado and boasting, for the man is not worthy of the name of philosopher, who publicly bears witness against us in matters which he does not understand, saying that the Christians are atheists and impious, and doing so to win favor with the deluded mob and to please them. For if he assails us without having read the teachings of Christ, he is thoroughly depraved and far worse than the illiterate, who often refrain from discussing or bearing false witness about matters that they do not understand. Or if he has read them and does not understand the majesty that is in them, or understanding it acts thus, that he may not be suspected of being such, that is, a Christian, he is far more base and thoroughly depraved, being conquered by illiberal and unreasonable opinion and fear."

Justin Martyr was very angry, and therefore he was a little less than fair to Crescens. Let us consider something for a moment. Justin Martyr says, "The ignorant don't talk this way about us. The people who are neighbors of some of our members don't slander us, and it's incredible that a philosopher should do so." A cynical philosopher is the last person we, today, would expect to accuse Christians of impiety and atheism. What then did these terms mean to the educated men of that day?

It is easy for us to discover what "piety" meant because we have a great deal of Roman literature on the subject. Piety meant something very different from what we normally understand by it — submission to the authority of the state. To the Romans, a pious man was a man who was faithful to every jot and tittle of Caesar's law. Obviously the Christians lacked such piety, because they insisted that Jesus Christ is Lord over Caesar. It did not help for some of them, like Tertullian, to argue in his appeal to the emperor, "But we are your best citizens. We are the best soldiers you have, the most honest taxpayers. Why, therefore, do you treat us like your enemies?" We could make the same appeal today.

As I appear in court after court, it is distressing to me to see Christians on trial, when we have so much lawlessness in the world. I became more than a little upset some time ago at the trial of two brothers, Wimbrick and Joseph Padgett, in Georgia. They were farmers, and they were Christian saints, with simplicity and clarity of faith and dedication that was profoundly moving. In fact, if I wanted a picture of the best of America and its character, I would have taken a picture of the Wimbrick and Joseph Padgett families.

But they were on trial for criminal charges, because they were teaching their children at home. The evidence, including that of the outgoing superintendent of schools, was clear-cut. These children were several years ahead of their peers in the local schooling system. At the end of my testimony I said, in answer to the State Attorney, that I found it very distressing to see men of this caliber on trial for criminal charges, when hoodlums were walking the streets and being turned loose in the courts on technicalities. I was very happy to see the judge pick up that statement, and he said, "I will write something and deliver it later, but I will say here and now that I regard this trial as a disgrace." He said to the State Attorney, "You know what you were doing when you brought people of this caliber into this court on criminal charges. I do not take kindly to it!"

Piety, then, in the Roman world, meant submission to the authority of the state. And the Christians were clearly guilty of a lack of piety, even though they were more law-abiding than most others.

Clement of Alexandria attempts to show in his writings that the Christian answering these charges — because such charges were commonplace generation after generation — is the one who alone is truly pious, because all authority comes from God. "And so true piety," he said, "is in relationship to almighty God."

What about the other charge, the charge of atheism? Of the charge of atheism, Clement of Alexandria declared in his *Miscellanies*, "He then who is persuaded that God is omnipotent and has learned the divine mysteries from His only begotten Son, how can he be an atheist? For he is an atheist who thinks that God does not exist, and he is superstitious who dreads the demons and who deifies all things both wood and stone and reduces to bondage the spirit and man who possesses the life of reason."

What Clement of Alexandria was doing was redefining atheism in terms of a biblical faith. And in order to understand the charge, we have to see it as the Romans saw it. We have evidence of this in a surviving account of the interrogation of several Christians. One of them, Dionysius, recorded the interrogation in a letter to Hermammon. Here is his account:

> Dionysius, Faustus, Maximus, Marcellus and Chiremone being arraigned, Amelianus the Roman official said, "I have reasoned verbally with you concerning the clemency which our rulers have shown to you. For they have given the opportunity to save yourselves, if you will turn to that which is according to nature and worship the gods that preserve their empire and forget those that are contrary to nature. What then do you say to this? For I do not think that you will be ungrateful for their kindness, since they would turn you to a better course."

Dionysius replied: "Not all people worship all gods, but each one those whom he approves. We therefore reverence and worship the one God, the maker of all, who has given the empire to the divine-favored Augustus Valerian and Gallianus, and we pray to Him continually for their empire, that it may remain unshaken."

Amelianus was ready to grant them clemency if they would depart from their atheistic kind of thinking and worship the gods of Rome. What were the gods of Rome? They were all deified men. Every emperor became a god by a declaration of the senate upon his death, and sometimes even before that. We know from Greek history, for example, that several cites claimed to have a relationship to Zeus: one as his birthplace, another as the location of his tomb, and still another for the fact that he supposedly ruled there for a time. So certain citizens could boast, "Zeus slept here on such and such an occasion." All the gods of the Greeks and Romans were deified men and thus part of the natural order. The deity implicit and inherent in all of nature came to focus in the social order and in the great men of that social order.

Such a philosophy is still very much with us today. The German philosopher, Hegel, who is the father of almost every political philosophy of the modern world — Marxism, Fascism, National Socialism, "democracy" — held that the state is God walking on earth and that the inherent divinity of nature comes to focus in the social order. Consequently, there is no God above and beyond the state. Hegel's philosophy led to positivism in law, which is the idea that law is what the state declares it to be.

This was simply a resurrection of the ancient faith of paganism of the Greco-Roman world. As this faith was beginning to revive, men looked back on the Christian centuries and called them "the Middle Ages." At first they called the period from the fall of Rome to the Renaissance "the Dark Ages." Then, of course, they found it very difficult to call these centuries "Dark," as they looked around Europe and saw the monuments of that time. So, little by little, they confined the Dark Ages to shorter and shorter periods of time, until now, when no reputable historian uses the term. Instead, they call it the Middle Ages, the middle period: a break in the continuity of history when mankind went astray and when, for a time, men — under the delusions of Christianity — left classical humanism. But, with the Renaissance civilization revived, and mankind was marching again! Such was the secular perspective — the state as God, walking on earth.

Let's return to Dionysius' account of the interrogation by Amelianus. Amelianus, the prefect, said to them, "But who forbids you to worship Him if He is a God, together with those who are gods by nature? For ye have been commanded to reverence the gods and the gods whom all know." Dionysius answered, "We worship no other." Amelianus then said, "I see that you are at once ungrateful and unsensible to the kindness of our sovereigns, wherefore ye shall not remain in this city. But ye shall be sent to a place called Cefro, for I have chosen this place at the command of our sovereigns (there was an emperor and a co-emperor). And it shall by no means be permitted you, or any others, either to hold assemblies or to enter into the so-called cemeteries. But if anyone shall be seen without the place which I have commanded or be found in any assembly, he shall bring peril on himself, for suitable punishment shall not fail. Go therefore where ye have been ordered." The "cemeteries" referred to the catacombs.

Among other things, we see here the totalitarian mentality. Amelianus felt he was being most gracious and generous in giving these believers a chance to submit. The modern state acts in the same way towards Christians who refuse to obey it. It feels it is being gracious by giving them a chance to submit. To Amelianus, atheism, as he plainly stated, was a disbelief in the natural gods — the forces of nature as they came to focus in the state. That was the issue.

Rome believed very profoundly in a philosophy of social order. Rome delighted in order. To effect that order, Rome had built up a most remarkable network of roads throughout the empire, so that the empire could be bound together by imperial law. It had remarkable aqueducts, again to bring order into every situation. It had legions posted all over the empire and a whole network of officials, again to effect order. Rome's belief was that order and morality were impossible without — to put it in modern terms — a policeman on every corner. Rome believed that if it withdrew the legions, the compulsive power of the state, total anarchy would result.

In a sense we agree with that. Paul says that the civil authorities and rulers are to be a terror to evildoers. But Rome believed that those authorities were gods walking on earth. They must therefore possess total authority, and the Empire must be the umbrella under which all things existed. All things must be under the state. This is diametrically opposed to the biblical concept that all things are under God, and it is not the imperial law but the law-word of God which is to govern the individual and the church, the school, the family, our vocations, society at large, and, finally, one form of government among many, civil government.

This doctrine was set forth early by a pope, Gelasius II, in a doctrine which became very popular, the concept of the two swords, the two great authorities by which God was going to rule. There is no question that the church very early took that commandment seriously. Let us remember that one of the most important passages in Scripture appears in 1 Corinthians 6 when Paul says,

> Dare any of you, having a matter against another, go to law before the unjust and not before the saints? Do ye not know that the saints shall judge the world? And if the world shall be judged by you, are ye unworthy to judge the smallest matters?

The word "judge" has reference to the Old Testament book of Judges, meaning "to govern." The saints are to govern the world, and they must begin by governing their own spheres.

Very early on, the church set up a government which adjudicated all controversies between members. Before long, pagans were coming to those courts until, by the time of the fall of Rome, because Rome had become so corrupt, the effectual government was the Christian court. The effective government of Europe, for three centuries almost entirely, and for six centuries to a large extent, was by church courts, and, I would submit, the best government it ever had. The church did not try to supplant the state. It tried to create, out of the ruins of Rome, a civil government which would minister in its appointed sphere. But the church itself took over a great deal of the government. There were courts to deal with ecclesiastical matters, family matters, civil matters, criminal matters, and so on.

We are seeing a resurrection of this in the United States today. It is primarily, although not entirely, under the auspices of a legal society. Arbitration councils have been set up in a number of communities. The Christians coming to these courts must agree to submit their case to a council of attorneys, and both parties sign a binding contract that they will abide by the results. In one modest-sized Western city recently, disputes involving a total of 26 million dollars were adjudicated by the courts without any problems in the course of one year. The saints are beginning to judge and to govern the world again.

Rome saw itself as the umbrella under which all things, including the church, had to exist. The church said, "We are not trying to arrogate or claim unduly any power that legitimately belongs to Caesar. We pray for Caesar." Rome felt that this was an impossibility. "These people," it said, "are talking about a power of government which comes from an invisible God and works invisibly in the individual. They are asking us to leave them alone in their churches and in their schools." Incidentally, the early church, following the synagogue pattern, was the school. It was also a library. Very significantly, the first churches built, contrary to an attitude which prevails in some church circles, were not simple structures, because they were the palaces of Christ the King! The sanctuary was built to resemble a throne-room. When the Scripture was read in those days, every member of the church stood, because the King was speaking. The Christians believed there was a government from God by His Holy Spirit at work in their lives and that there was a standard superior to the Roman imperial law which governed their churches and schools: the Word of God, the "canon," or the "rule," they called it.

Rome felt that there could be no morality apart from the legions and the Roman authorities maintaining order and control. With that faith, Rome began to disintegrate. Even as they were persecuting Christians, the Roman circuses were becoming a dominant feature on the Roman scene. Rome had begun to fear the people, and it was using handouts to keep them in line. Bread and circuses were the only way to keep the masses from revolting. By approximately A.D. 275, it had reached the point where, not only was there welfare for all those who claimed it, but, to remove the trauma of having to apply for welfare, the emperor decreed it would be an hereditary right belonging to all children of welfare recipients. The next year he had nothing more to give them, and so they killed him!

The modern state is pursuing the same course. It is offering more and more handouts to a people it cannot control by its law-word. It cannot make them over into godly, law-abiding citizens. Yet it is turning on the Christians and saying, "You are out of line. You are destroying our law and order. Your schools and your churches are an offense to us. What we are trying to do is to create a stable society, a culture in which there is a common moral standard."

"You," said Rome to the Christians, "are atheists because the idea of any God over and beyond the state, any God over and beyond nature, is a myth." Is that not the attitude we face today from the world?

The authority of the state was set forth as the ultimate natural order. While we cannot speak with authority about Crescens, with whom Justin Martyr was upset, we know that most of the pagan philosophers read the Bible with a sense of awe. For them, the only moral force which was tenable was the fear of the state. No remote, "unnatural" (from their perspective, and from our perspective "supernatural") power, the triune God, could restrain man. To deny the force of the natural order and its status as the ultimate moral, legal, and governmental order was atheism. What else, they held, could make men behave?

The subject of the atheism of the early church opens up an element which I think should be of interest, and emphasizes the centrality of the doctrine of the Spirit in our thinking. We believe at Chalcedon that the first great statement made with regard to the Holy Spirit after His role in creation is that He is the Spirit of wisdom and of understanding. We are also told, by James the Apostle, that there is one thing we can all have without question if we ask God for it. All the other gifts of God and of the Spirit are conditional, but there is one gift we could all have just for the asking. It is obvious when we look at our world today, and especially the church, that very few people do ask for it. It is wisdom. "If any of you lack wisdom, let him ask, and it shall be given unto you."

It is important for us to recognize the centrality of this doctrine, because it tells us that there is a power who is a Person at work in the world, who provides more order than the state can and who Himself, as one of the triune Godhead, ordained the life of the state. When the state separates itself from the triune God, it signs its own death warrant. As that Godhead speaking as Wisdom said of old, "He that sinneth against me wrongeth his own soul. All they that hate me love death."

A love of death is very prevalent the world over. Today we are in the death throes of humanistic statism all over the world. The only question is, "Are we going to be a part of that fearful suicide?" God's Word says, "Come out from among them and be separate." We shall establish our churches, our schools, our families, our callings, in terms of the sovereign Word of God, and where it is necessary to be obedient to human authorities, we shall be obedient. But where we must obey God rather than men, we obey God and God alone. We recognize that the only true strength of a society, its only source of moral order, is not from the state. The state cannot provide moral order. Only God, through His faithful church, through His Spirit, through His Word, can give us that order.

It is that order the world is desperately in need of today. The crisis of order is a crisis of major proportions. It haunts the Soviet Union. They are increasingly unable to handle their own young. The son of a friend of mine went into the Soviet Union during a tour of Europe, on his own with his Volkswagen, and very quickly found that he was absorbed into the community of the sons of the elite in Moscow. He found that it was very much like the world of nightclubs here: a passionate attachment to rock and roll, with the ultimate status symbol being patched and faded blue jeans, and no concern with anything other than personal pleasure.

Productivity is falling in the Soviet Union year by year. Productivity is falling throughout the Western world. Men are functioning less and less in terms of producing, building, and developing, and more and more in terms of consuming, enjoying, and withdrawing from a world of work and responsibility. We are indeed in critical times, when the world is collapsing all around us and when what we need is that which Rome called the "atheism" of the early church: a recognition that God alone is Lord, that He is sovereign over us and that, "Except the Lord build the house, they labor in vain that build it."

Chapter Two

The Loss of Justice

In 1971 a European scientist named Roberto Vacca wrote a book entitled *The Coming Dark Age*. Writing from the standpoint of science and technology, he predicted the forthcoming breakdown of urban life. He said that, because of a combination of growing illiteracy, of taxation which was destroying the ability of systems to renew themselves, and many other things, the major systems in the Western World — transit, garbage collection, telephone, power, and the mails — would break down. He felt that between 1985 and 1994 there would be major collapses in those areas of technology which sustain civilized life. His forecast intentionally omitted the possibility of war, which would of course accelerate this collapse.

Vacca's perspective — that we face the coming of a Dark Age — has been echoed by a number of other scholars. All have a common premise: namely, that the "Dark Age" may lie ahead of us. The fact is that we are now in the world's darkest "Dark Age."

The term "Dark Age" originally comes from Christian writers in the early church. They spoke of the Dark Ages as any part of history, any part of the world, which was outside of Christ. So the Dark Age is out there in the streets of Sydney, Los Angeles, Chicago, San Francisco, London, Berlin, Paris, and all the world. Moreover, one English scholar, Gil Elliot, in his book *The*

Twentieth Century Book of the Dead, gives us some amazing data. According to Elliot, in no other era of history and in no other century has a higher percentage of mankind been killed by war, by revolution, by man-enforced famine, in slave labor camps, and so on. A higher proportion of mankind, he said, has died in this century than in any other era of human history. This is the real "Dark Age."

The data recorded in his book, incidentally, concluded with the beginning of the Sixties. Since then we have learned so much more about the vast numbers who died as a result of the Chinese revolution. We have learned that in Africa there have been systematic massacres of Christians by the hundreds of thousands, and that in Cambodia the Khmer Rouge systematically eliminated fifty-percent of the population. I have talked to two survivors of this slaughter, and the categories which governed the policy of extermination were as follows: anyone who lived in the city and had a knowledge of urban life; anyone who had any education and could read or write (which meant he had ideas that would not readily be eradicated by the Marxist leaders); anyone who had ever traveled abroad; anyone who had worked for the old government or had a relative who had worked for them; and finally and supremely, any and all who were Christian. Half the population of Cambodia died.

The Dark Age is there all around us. Yet, when he dealt with the data in the early Sixties, Elliot had to suppress a question which came up in his mind. As a good liberal he opposed the idea that sin had anything to do with it, or that man could be regarded as depraved. But it left him with no way of accounting for what had happened.

The kind of thing that Elliot revealed through statistics should not surprise us, given the history of Western thought beginning with the Enlightenment and especially with the French Revolution. At the beginning of the last century, Max Stirner, in his book *The Ego and His Own*, called for a militant anarchism and challenged all his fellow-atheists, accusing them of being closet Christians. He said, Which of you has the courage to sleep with his daughter, sister, or mother? Until you do, you are closet Christians. Stirner's writings were revived at the beginning of the Sixties and were very influential in the world-wide student movement. Nietzsche was another who summoned mankind to "live beyond good and evil."

In 1973, Walter Kauffmann, a Princeton philosopher who died prematurely not long ago, published his book entitled, *Without Guilt and Justice*. Kauffmann's thesis was simply this: guilt is a religious concept, and it has reference to the God of Scripture. Therefore, to deal in civil society with questions of guilt and innocence is to presuppose the existence of the God of Scripture. And this, he said, we cannot do. Similarly, we must abandon any concept of justice or injustice, the will of a supernatural God — something which we know is a nonsensical idea. And, therefore, we must reorder society beyond the conception of good and evil, beyond guilt or innocence, beyond justice and injustice.

Significantly, on the last page of his study, this philosopher, Hegelian to the core, cited Scripture. He pronounced Genesis 3:1-5, the Tempter's program as advanced to Eve:

> Ye shall be as god, every man his own god, knowing, determining for yourself what is good and evil.

He concludes, that the world then was not ready for this gospel.

We have today the consequences of generations of this kind of thinking. We have Paul Hoffman, an American writer, in 1974 titling his account of the life of a prominent criminal lawyer in the United States, *What the hell is justice?* — a quotation from a criminal lawyer. This is what our culture is asking. As a result, there is a widespread sense of the loss of justice.

We have to agree with Kauffmann. Guilt and innocence, justice and injustice, have reference to the God of Scripture. If you eliminate faith in that God, if you become systematically humanist, you must abandon any thought of justice or injustice. God is the source of true justice. The decay of justice means, therefore, the decay of true religion. Unless justice is grounded in the very nature and being of God, it is a peripheral and unnecessary concept at best: justice becomes merely someone's ideal, or idea, and not the nature of reality. Justice is only truly important to those who believe that it represents the very nature of God.

Early in the 1960s I was at the William Volker Foundation. I was then living not far from the University of Stanford and doing a great deal of my research at the Stanford University Library. I had occasion at that time to meet a prominent, classical American economist who was very conservative. While not a Christian, he was very much given to the old liberal standards: a belief in freedom, in justice, and so on. He was never able, to his dying day, to get over his horror, when speaking to the students at Stanford, at their rejection of the concept of freedom as invalid. They were not interested. "If you had spoken about justice," I told him, "you would have gotten the same response." Because their concern was with a revolution which gave them things, they rejected out of hand the idea of liberty. And they would have similarly rejected justice, because it deals with a spiritual realm.

To deny justice is to deny God. Moreover, we have failed to see the meaning of justice as it relates to God and to us. A century ago, an English theologian and Old Testament scholar, Girdlestone, called attention to the sad fact that the English language had two words which meant the same thing. One had been appropriated by the churches and the other by the state, and the two words had come to mean two different things. Those two words are "righteousness" and "justice," but their meaning is one and the same. When the Bible speaks about the righteousness of God, it is talking about the justice of God. When we are told that we are created in the image of God — which is knowledge, righteousness, holiness, and dominion — we are told by Scripture that we are created in righteousness or justice. We are told that Christ restores this fallen image, so that we are restored to our creation mandate, which is to exercise dominion and to subdue the earth in terms of this image of God in us: justice, knowledge, righteousness, holiness.

Thus, justice or righteousness is of major concern to us. It sets forth the nature of God. If we lose sight of the fact that justice is a concern of Christians, we are surrendering the world to the enemy. And too many churchmen, by becoming antinomian or anti-law, are in effect denying God, because God is the Lord over all things, including the state. The state has as much a duty to manifest the righteousness of God as does the church — as do you and I. Therefore, in every area, it is the standard of God's righteousness, God's justice, God's law, which must be our canon. As Isaiah 8:20 says:

> To the law and to the testimony: if they speak not according to this word, it is because there is no light in them.

I was very impressed a few years ago in reading a book which, while otherwise generally worthless, brought out the fact that modern man has a "compulsive coolness" where things of importance are concerned. He can get excited about rock and roll and about a great many trivialities, but where the essentials of our civilization and the essentials of the faith are concerned, there is a "compulsive coolness." This is an aspect of a general cynicism, a preference for things one can despise and look down upon. The sad fact is that the church, where it approaches the things of God, has this same "compulsive coolness." It has no zeal for God's righteousness. It has no concern for God's law. It has failed to require that the state be a ministry of justice.

I want to emphasize that it is *a* ministry, not *the* ministry, of justice. Every area of life and thought must manifest the righteousness of God. Government is not limited to the state. It begins with the self-government of the Christian man. It includes the self-government of the family, of the church, of the school, of vocations, of society at large. All these things govern us in every area. Justice and righteousness must be manifest. If we limit justice to the state, it means that justice has gone out of our lives. It must be the life of all men and all society, and it begins with us, with our lives and with our conduct of the things which are ours.

Tithing, by the way, is a form of justice. It is giving to God His tax. Today, of course, people are not concerned about robbing God. Nor are they in too many cases unduly concerned with the killing of unborn babies, with giving license to homosexuality, and more. Should we be surprised that this age attacks the church and the ministries of the church, such as the Christian school? Moreover, we see the concept of justice itself subjected to massive attack. Modern-day law schools have attempted to separate justice from morality.

In the 1920's, John W. Burgess, a very prominent political conservative in the United States, a legal scholar and professor of political science at Columbia University in New York, wrote a book entitled *The Sanctity of Law*. He spent the entire book doing two things: separating law from God and from morality and saying that it expressed the will of the state; and insisting at the same time on the sanctity of the law, because what the state wills is of necessity "holy." It should not surprise us, given such a fact in legal tradition, that we have the problems we do.

The state can only administer justice when the state itself is under God, and when, most importantly, the people are under God. The state which denies God denies justice. But the modern state sees itself as a lawmaker. Lawmaking is an attribute of deity. The source of law in any system is the god of that system. Originally, in terms of the English tradition, the American colonies and subsequently the states did not speak of having legislatures. That is a relatively recent usage. They called the body the House of Burgesses, or the General Assembly, and so on. It did not exist in order to make laws, but rather to assist in bringing the will of the people to bear on what the civil magistrates did to further justice in the community.

Now, of course, such bodies have become lawmakers. They make more laws than any of us can begin to read. Each session of the legislatures and Congress, as well as the bureaucratic agencies, passes enough laws each year to fill a barn. We are faced with a great mass of fiat law.

The word "fiat" comes from the first chapter of Genesis — "fiat lux." "Let there be light!" "Fiat" means the creative act whereby, with a mere word, something can be brought into existence. As a result, we have today, in virtually every modern state, fiat money — paper money. As Von Mises said, it is a remarkable fact that every civil government in the world can take perfectly good paper and turn it into worthless money. We have a proliferation of fiat laws — laws which have no relationship to God's righteousness.

For example, in 1930 it was illegal to walk down the streets of the United States carrying a bottle of wine, but not illegal to carry a bar of gold. Five years later, the wine was legal and the gold was illegal. Neither piece of legislation had anything to do with justice. It represented the fiat will of the state. We are increasingly seeing the fiat will of the state become law, with the consequent breakdown of law all around us.

This "virus" goes back to ancient Greece. Greek philosophy held that there was an independent realm of values which was a realm of forms, ideas, or pure reason. It held that an elite group — philosopher-kings — could incarnate this reason, and thus the universals, too, were incarnate in the philosopher-kings: therefore they would rule with perfect justice. The virus of that faith has infected the Western world. The French Revolution was an attempt to establish it. One of our staff members, Otto Scott, has written a book on Robespierre entitled, *Robespierre, the Voice of Virtue*. Robespierre saw himself as precisely that — the voice of reason and virtue — as does the dictatorship in the Soviet Union, which believes in its own infallibility. It is infallible because it incarnates the voice of reason, the incarnate deity in all of being.

Autonomous reason can thus remake the world after its own image, and all who oppose such a state are opposing the voice of reason. The result has been the control of education, terrorism, moves to destroy the family and the church, biological engineering, and much more. The goal is to remake man in the image of the elite planners, and the result is massive injustice. Just as for us the source of all meaning is the triune God, so for these men it is the state. And the state now is in the process of definition, of redefining all things. Perhaps it is not as bad in Australia and New Zealand as it is in the United States, where the Internal Revenue Service can look you in the face and, contrary to the plain meaning of the language as you read it, tell you that something does not mean what you think it means. Rather, it means what they *say* it means! They define the language, and as they redefine it, it takes on their meaning. It is interesting, too, that if they assess you something for taxes they feel are due to them, they will tell you — using the language of God — that you have thirty or sixty "days of grace" to pay it. The modern state is in the business of redefining the meaning of all things.

Recently I was speaking to a very dear friend of mine, Bill Richardson, a California State Senator. He commented with some exasperation on what he had been experiencing in the State Senate. He said, "Do you know, I do believe they are going to eliminate every crime by redefinition. One of these days I expect them to eliminate rape by redefining it as 'unilateral sex.'"

Moreover, if we do not begin with the justice of God, the righteousness of God, then we begin with the ostensible justice or righteousness of the state. There is no appeal beyond the state, and what the state declares to be law is right.

In 1975, some pro-life people, anti-abortionists, cornered then-senator John Tunney of the United States Senate in Southern California, and challenged him on the morality of abortion. He defended it as moral. "On what grounds?," he was asked. "On the ground that it is legal." "Well," they asked, "if a majority of the American people pass a law tomorrow demanding the legislation of theft, would theft then be moral?" He said, "Yes — because it will then be legal!"

This is the present direction of all humanistic thinking the world over, to identify the will of the state as something beyond which there can be no appeal. If we deny God's justice as basic to the life of man, we deny that appeal. We say there is no Supreme Court of almighty God to which men can make appeal.

We face that problem today in some forthcoming court cases. There is an abortion clinic picketing case in North Carolina. Doctors are now suing those who picket their abortion clinics with signs reading, "Abortion is Murder." This is slander, they say, as they go to court. Since abortion is legal, to refer to it as murder and to call it immoral is legally wrong. They are suing, I believe, for something like a million dollars in damages.

The sad fact is this: if we do not recognize God's justice as above and over man and the state — the church, the family, the school, every area of life and thought — then these people are right. We have withdrawn God's rule, His sovereignty, His justice, from that area of life. Proverbs 12:28 tells us:

> In the way of righteousness or justice is life; and in the pathway thereof there is no death.

The loss of justice is the key fact of our time. It rests in a loss of faith in the triune God and in the will of man to be his own god. But the penalty for sin is always death, whether for men or for civilizations or for civil governments. Christ our Redeemer has called us to holiness and to righteousness or justice, and only through His Word can we find the word for all men and all nations.

Chapter Three

Intercession

It is necessary for us as we approach the Word of God, to understand the context of every sentence thereof. Paul's letters, for example, were not written because he sat down and said, "I am now going to tell the churches what I think they need to hear." On the contrary. He was answering urgent questions from the church on matters of grave moment to them.

When we read Romans 13, we need to ask ourselves what question was asked of Paul. The answer is an obvious one, because at the time the great issue developing, which was to tear the church at its vitals for several centuries, as persecutions struck and as some compromised and left, was this: "Who is the Lord, Christ or Caesar?" Caesar claimed to be the lord, the sovereign. The church declared that "Jesus Christ is Lord," and this was the baptismal confession. So it was that the Christians raised the question, "If Jesus is Lord, and if Caesar is not lord, should we ever obey Caesar? Have we any obligation then toward Caesar?"

It was in answer to this question that Paul wrote what he did in Romans 13. What he said in effect was that the state is a ministry under God. The word he uses in the Greek is "diakonos," a deacon, a servant of God. We obey the state because our belief — to translate what he says into modern terminology — is not in salvation by revolution but salvation by regeneration. And so we obey. We remind all of the role of the state as a ministry, a terror to evildoers. We are subject, not because Caesar requires it, but for conscience's sake, conscience in relationship to our Lord.

The same is true of Paul's words in 1 Timothy 2:1 and 2. These verses are very much abused. What Paul says is this:

> I exhort therefore that, first of all, supplications, prayers, intercessions, and giving of thanks be made for all men; for kings, and for all that are in authority; that we may lead a quiet and peaceable life in all godliness and honesty.

We are to be intercessors for all men, including kings.

This is not to advocate an unconditional submission to civil authorities. As a matter of fact, this text was actually an offense to Rome and an occasion for conflict. Stuart Perowne, in his study of Christ and the church and the relationship of these things to the Caesars, speaks of the conflict as follows: "Of the attitude of the Christians to the state, this was in brief that, while they were ready and anxious to pray *for* Caesar, as their Master had taught them, they refused to pray *to* him. This attitude simply confirmed the belief that they were a seditious and subversive organization."

Do you see the difference? The church gave offense to the Roman Empire, because instead of praying *to* divine Augustus, they prayed *for* him and for all men. This put Caesar on a level with all men, even the humblest within his realm, and to Rome this was an offense. When we are commanded to pray for rulers, the commandment is to pray for them as we pray for all men, for their redemption, that they might be faithful to the Lord, and discharge their calling as God requires of them.

Those of you who know the story of *Fiddler on the Roof* may recall the incident where the students ask the old rabbi, "Rabbi, how should we pray for the czar?" And the old rabbi says, "Pray that God bless the czar, and keep him far from us."

There was a touch of this in the early church, although their attitude was basically much more positive. They were to pray for rulers, "that we may lead a quiet and peaceable life in all godliness and honesty." There was a recognition that civil order and peace are dependent upon the just exercise of authority by those who are in positions of leadership. The church was to give thanks for all good government which a civil ruler provides, and to pray for God's guidance for as well as His judgment upon those who go astray. Therefore our prayers for civil authorities, as commanded by Paul, involve intercession for them also. This in itself is a very significant fact. One who intercedes for another thereby has a greater position of power.

A year ago this last January, Mr. Ball, myself, and six others were in the White House for a meeting. We had asked a White House aide to set up the meeting by interceding for us, that such a meeting could be held. You appeal to someone who has power to intercede for you. This means that Paul was saying that all Christians have a position of great power, greater power than the Caesars, when they come before the Throne of almighty God as intercessors.

Moreover, the Greek word for intercession is a technical term. It means one who is the "go-between," between the people and the king. Paul was saying, "Caesar is a needy soul. As Christians we are to intercede for him with the King of kings. We are to be involved in continual intercession because, through Christ, we have continual access with Him who is able to save them to the uttermost, that come unto God by Him, seeing He ever liveth to make intercession for them."

What Paul is speaking about, in his letter to the Church at Rome and to Timothy, is not to be misinterpreted as indicating that the Christian simply submits without question to the state, no matter what the situation, and sees himself as duty-bound to obey. No, we are commanded to obey, but we must obey God rather than men. We have a greater position than all kings and emperors in that we are all, through the power of prayer, intercessors.

One pastor in Georgia, Reverend Robert McCurdy, had problems with the Internal Revenue Service. His church, a very large and well-known church with a parochial school of some 700 students, was sent a letter which demanded that they submit all their records, all the data concerning their membership, how much everyone had given, what expenditures were and to whom they were paid, and the Constitution, bylaws, and other documents of the church. The final sentence in the letter said, "Answer within 30 days."

Bob McCurdy wrote back: "We are under Christ and not under you. Why are you asking us these questions? P.S. I am sending you a copy of our only Constitution. It is called the Holy Bible."

He received a stiff note in return, indicating that this was not regarded as a suitable document. However, in the church bulletin, Pastor McCurdy called attention to the situation and asked the congregation to pray that God would abolish the I.R.S. Apparently the I.R.S. — as it does with other groups — had someone placed on the mailing list who provided them with all the mailings, because they sent a very angry note of protest about that prayer request. The I.R.S. did not regard it as a suitable subject of prayer.

To intercede with a higher power is our calling. The higher power is God almighty, not the state. But today it is increasingly evident that men regard the state as the supreme power, the higher authority.

Segundo, one of the liberal theologians, very influential in the Americas, has written, "We give the name of socialism to a political regime in which the ownership of the means of production is removed from individuals and handed over to higher institutions whose concern is the common good." As Segundo develops this point, it is clear that there is simply one higher institution which is higher than all else and is over all men and all agencies, and it is the state. Segundo's thesis, and that of all liberal theologians, is that the state is the transcendental institution, the agency which is above all principalities and powers, which replaces God and should replace Him in the hearts and minds of men.

Only the state is deemed to be capable of exercising an interest for the common good, to be above partial and limited interests, and like God to be always just in its decisions. All we have to do, of course, is to look at the morning paper to know otherwise. The state is neither infallible nor incorruptible, nor any better than its citizens. But this is the concept of the state which is very much with us and which is a product of a great deal of modern philosophy, such as Hegelianism, as well as being rooted deeply in antiquity.

Many years ago, an English scholar, W.W. Willoughby, summing up the ancient Greek concept of the state as the ultimate or final order, wrote: "In such a political philosophy as this, the idea that the state existed solely or even chiefly for the protection of the private rights of its citizens, of course found no place. Rather, it was held that without the state the individual would have no rights at all, not even natural or moral rights, for without the education and order which the state affords, he would have neither the disposition nor the opportunity to lead a moral, rational life."

A further consequence of this idea of the scope of the state was to make of politics and ethics practically one science. In the writings of Plato, the two were completely identified. Aristotle distinguished between them, but, in conformity with the principles we have been stating, he made politics the master science, with ethics as one of its subsidiaries. Thus he explicitly declares his ethics to be a political treatise and to be but an introduction to his treatise on politics proper.

This idea is very much with us as we see the state increasingly claiming jurisdiction over every area of life and thought, as though it were from God; as though all rights, all moral principles, stemmed from itself; as though there could be no dissent from the state without violating some divine moral premise. But it is only the Lord God of hosts who can command such an allegiance.

Moreover, as Willoughby went on to say, "It was not so much that the state interfered in almost everything, but rather that everything was absorbed in the state. Religion was the state's religion, and anyone who announced new gods had to drain the fatal cup. The family was only a means to the end of the state. The state might prevent trade and fetter the full activities of the economy of individuals. It acknowledged no society but itself. That state was only the logical consequence of the same political ideas which proscribed to music its melodies, to instruments their tunes and even ventured to forbid the Hellenes to read Homer." Willoughby's point was well taken. Everything was absorbed into the state, and man had neither life nor freedom apart from it. The presupposition was the infallibility of the state and the imbecility of all who opposed it.

Today we have a like doctrine. It has its developments, it has been refined at certain points, but essentially to deny the supremacy of the state is regarded today as invalid. The state is the great moral premise. Why? Because, since Rousseau, we have seen an identification of all moral authority with the people — the voice of the people is the voice of God ("vox populi, vox dei") — and the state as the voice of the people.

As a result, we have a deification of the people and of the people's state. The Marxist countries call themselves the People's Republic of Such-and-such — the German People's Federal Republic, or the People's Republic of North Korea or China, or whatever the case may be. In the Western democracies, the appeal is again to the people. We have that kind of situation which Lewis J. Howell has described as follows: "Today, when the Premier of the Soviet Union addresses a communication to the President of the United States, he undertakes to express the view of the Soviet people on the matter in question. When the President of the United States replies, he gives the answer of the American people to the contents of the Premier's note. At San Francisco in 1945, at the founding of the United Nations, 60 individual persons, vested with the authority of as many sovereign states, some of them what we call dictatorships and a few what we call liberal democracies, drew up and agreed upon a document that begins, 'We, the peoples of the United Nations....'"

What does this mean? The greatest form of political quackery today is to clothe oneself in the name of the people. The politicians who claim to express the will of the people mean by it that, if you disagree with them, you are opposed to all the people and you are not one of the people. They imply that they somehow incarnate themselves the will of the people, which *ipso facto* has all moral force and all authority. But the voice of the prophets and the voice of Scripture is, "Thus saith the Lord...," not, "Thus saith the people...." "The people" do not exist. It is simply a collective noun, one which unscrupulous individuals use to give themselves a borrowed authority.

We must say to the people, to the People's Republics of this earth, and to the self-styled voices of the people, "Thus saith the Lord...." We must say that we are the people of the King, and anyone can belong to or, be one of the people of the King. We are intercessors, and therefore we are the people of power. Power does not belong to a mythical "people," but to God, and it flows from Him to all the world.

Men like Robespierre could say that all is permitted to those who act in the name of the people. Because of that we had the terror of the guillotine.

Today we have those who, in the name of the people, insist that the church and its ministries must be controlled. Today we have countries where, in the name of the people, Christianity has been suppressed and martyrdom is the order of the day. Very few people realize, because we no longer hear about it, that the persecution of Christians in the Soviet Union has been stepped up in recent years. It has been stepped up because Christians are growing in such great numbers. The Soviets are finding that, when they locate a church and raid it and arrest most of its members, if two or three escape, each of them goes his own way and starts another congregation. They destroy one only to have three new ones spring up!

They are finding that, whereas twenty years ago these people simply bowed their heads and took their sentence when arrested, they are now speaking up to the prosecutors and to the courts in the name of almighty God. They are speaking in the name of the Lord who is Lord over them, they declare, and who will judge their judges. It is no wonder the authorities are stepping up the persecution. They are recognizing the power which is growing in their midst.

The Christians offended Rome by praying to God, not to Caesar, and by praying for Caesar. Humanism is offended if we do not invoke the name of the people, or surrender to the name and the power of the state. I have been in courtrooms where Christians on trial have been rebuked by the court for quoting Scripture. In fact, when Mr. Ball and I were in Michigan, the judge, who, to the amazement of everyone, finally ruled in our favor, nonetheless expressed exasperation with the pastors and Christian school teachers because they were quoting Scripture. He said, "I do not want to hear any more Bible, please!"

His attitude was understandable, because to invoke Scripture is to invoke a higher law. It is to declare that there is a Higher Court. It is an implicit appeal for intercession by God, whose law is also on trial in all such cases.

We face a problem today, because we again have a pagan doctrine of intercession spreading all around us. "Do you have a problem?," people are asked. "Why, go to the welfare agency, or go to Medicare, or go to the Government Center at the County seat. They have someone who will take care of you." The young people in our state schools are encouraged to believe that they can find intercession with any of these authorities in problems with their parents. They are asked, "Are your parents requiring you to go to Sunday school? That's unfair. Are they requiring you to take part in family worship? That's unfair. If you will go to the counselor, we can do something for you. Seek intercession from the state."

This is a religious matter. Intercession is a religious doctrine. In intercession we always go to the higher power, and as intercessors we must recognize that the higher power is not Caesar, who is under the law of Jesus Christ, but is the triune God. As His intercessors, we have a responsibility to exercise His government. He requires of us that we rear our children in the nurture and admonition of the Lord. They cannot be reared in terms of that commandment if they are given to humanistic schools, where the content of learning is anti-Christian at heart. Our work as intercessors mandates therefore that in every area of life and thought we take over the ministry of compassion, as we deal one with another, as members one of another, ministering to human need in every area.

Paul began by declaring that Christians were to intercede by praying for rulers. The early church saw this as a ministry whereby, as intercessors with the King, they communicated the grace and the mercy of God to all peoples. So they had a mission to everyone, believer and unbeliever — the ministry of grace with the Gospel, a ministry of compassion whereby they ministered to the human needs of the community, a ministry of missions to those who were near and to those who were far. This was because they were intercessors. They brought the Word of God and the life God has ordained for man to bear upon every area of life and thought. Step by step, they replaced bread and circuses with a ministry to the whole man. This is how hospitals were born in Europe, and universities, schools of all kinds, missions to lepers, missions to the people on the frontiers and beyond. It was seen as an aspect of the ministry of intercession, by interceding to God for all and by carrying out the commandment of God to all.

Today, all over the world, we have a modern state which is playing God. It is doing so because by default we have allowed it to take over one area after another, as we have abandoned our ministries in those areas. We need to begin resuming that ministry. It begins by praying *for,* not *to,* all authorities, and then exercising the authority which is ours in Jesus Christ over every area of life and thought.

Chapter Four

The Law and Justice

How do you answer someone who questions a number of spiritual things, such as theonomy and the resurrection? The answer is, you do not. Let me illustrate.

Almost forty years ago, I was a missionary on an Indian reservation in an isolated area of northeastern Nevada, a hundred miles from any bus, town, or trainline. I had the Indian reservation, a sheep town of about a hundred people eighty miles North, and a little mining camp off the edge of the reservation, to minister to.

One man in that mining camp was very eager to see me. He was starved for companionship. I was amazed to find that he was quite well-educated. He knew both classical and New Testament Greek. So he welcomed me and wanted me to stop by as often as possible, which I did about once a month. The first time I was there, he rejected any approach in terms of the faith. He said, "I don't believe. I regard the Bible as a full of a lot of nonsense, such as the story of Jonah and the whale."

I said, "John, let me tell you something. There is a book, now rather rare, which describes the experiences of American whalers in the last century. Several of them were washed overboard or fell overboard and were swallowed by either a whale or a great fish of some sort. A day or two later, when that particular creature was harpooned and taken aboard, they were still alive and were rescued. It is a matter of historical record in the last century."

"On top of that," I continued, "there is the interesting fact of a Mediterranean medallion dated approximately the same time as, or slightly thereafter, the day described in Jonah. This medallion commemorates a strange event and is very different from everything else we have. It shows a giant fish coming close to the shore and regurgitating a man. That seems to indicate that perhaps there is something to the story, wouldn't you agree?"

"Well, yes, I agree," he said. "But there is this about the Bible...." And he went on to something else. I found that I was answering one objection after another and citing historical data. About a year or so later, he raised the issue of Jonah and the whale again. I had, by that time, grown slightly wiser, and I said, "John, I am beginning to realize something. Your problem is not Jonah and the whale, nor anything else in the Bible. Your problem is that you are a sinner, and you are going to erect every kind of intellectual barrier to conceal that fact. Let's get to the real problem that you have with the Bible, the fact that it says you're a sinner and you won't admit it." With that, he made it clear that he did not want me to come back!

Do not waste time on arguments. Man's problem is not intellectual: it is religious. This is man's problem in every area of life and thought. That is why, when we approach the subject of the law, we are again dealing inescapably with a religious fact. All law is inescapably moral. To summarize that premise very briefly: all law condemns something which is regarded as bad and protects other things as good. Moreover, morality is an aspect of religion. You cannot escape the fact that, when you enact a legal system, you have an establishment of religion. Every legal system in the world is an establishment of a religion. It may be Christianity, or it may be Humanism or Buddhism or Islam or Shintoism, but every legal system represents a moral and a theological structure.

The idea that we cannot legislate morality is nonsense. That is all we can legislate. Whatever we do legislate represents a moral judgment, whether it be good or bad, Christian or non-Christian. This is why, whenever a new religion enters a country, it is opposed. If it begins to be successful, it is persecuted because it is a threat to the foundations of the state. Rome knew what it was doing. Rome recognized that Christianity had a different moral system. It had a different sovereign, Jesus Christ, not Caesar. Rome recognized that its law was premised, not on the word of Caesar or the Roman Senate, but on the Word of God. Therefore, the Empire felt it was urgently necessary to oppose Christianity.

When Rome finally accepted Christianity, it was a pragmatic acceptance. The emperors did everything to undermine the faith. Every state must come to terms with religion, because a non-religious state cannot exist. This does not necessitate the establishment of a particular church. It does mean that the laws and the character of the state inescapably reflect a religious faith. This is why one of the great American Supreme Court justices, Justice Story, made it clear — even though he was for his day a liberal and the head of the Unitarian Association of America — that a very strict biblical faith was, in essence, the common law of the United States. It provided the basis of our legal system.

But, of course, the problem now is that the United States has been in the process of changing its foundation, as have other countries, from a Christian to a humanistic one. All too often, not only our schools — which are establishments of religion, humanistic religion — but also our courts reflect this new religion.

Incidentally, there are any number of books which openly avow in their training of public school teachers that they are to teach values, and that these values are humanistic. When I testified for the churches of Michigan, I took to the stand with me a book edited by one of the Michigan educators, entitled *A Humanistic Source-book in Education.* Its objective was to train teachers to inculcate humanistic values in their students — plainly religious teaching. I submit that state schools are unquestionably given to a religious faith, and that faith is in conflict with and at war with the Christian faith.

Law is inescapably religious. Law, moreover, inescapably reflects a concept of justice or righteousness. Justice is inseparable from true law. If the law does not embody justice, the state and the society are unstable and will inevitably collapse. If the law does not embody God's law, God's righteousness, God's justice, it will in some form embody that of man. But what happens when man says, "Go to now, we will make laws out of our own reasoning, out of our own resources." The problem is that man is fallen. How can fallen man provide justice? He is a sinner! Anything he enacts will reflect his nature, his particular interests. As a result, the law will reflect a class interest or particular interest, and it will not be justice.

Those who say we should be content as Christians to stay in our churches and allow the state to give us humanistic laws are saying in effect that we can have a righteous social order based upon the premise of fallen man. They are saying that the Tower of Babel could have succeeded and is going to succeed some day.

However, unless the Lord build the house, they labor in vain that build it. What we have all over the world today is the attempt by fallen man to create a Tower of Babel in the state, and, in the United Nations, to create it on an international basis. But if fallen man can legislate and work justice or righteousness in one area in the state, why then can he not work righteousness in every other area and save himself? This is the implication of rejecting God's law in favor of man's law. If man's righteousness can manifest itself in spite of the fact that he is fallen, and if man can show forth true justice in one area, why not in every area?

The simple fact is that, in the long history of man, man's law has always been oppressive, evil, and tyrannical. When man seeks to legislate apart from God, he legislates his sin. In the United States, originally there were no legislatures. There was a General Assembly, a House of Burgesses, and other such bodies which met together in order to help expedite the enforcement of a Christian order, a Christian structure, and righteousness in society. Step by step these were converted into legislatures where men felt they could effect righteousness on their own apart from God.

Humanistic man conjures up some human entity which can decree justice. The divine right of kings was such a doctrine. Today we have the doctrine of the people somehow embodying justice. It seems that all we have to do is to allow the people to express themselves and we will have justice. The poet Carl Sandburg wrote a book with the title, *The People, Yes*, implying that there mere voice of the people would effect righteousness.

Let me cite Dr. Howell on the subject of the people: "Both the liberal and Jacobean procedures are based on the premise that among the forms of being in the existential world, there is a personal entity called 'the people.' Orthodox Marxists conceive of this entity as singular: a world-wide social class which will be, at last, when its enemies have been eliminated and will comprehend the entire population of mankind. Nationalists conceive of it a plural, as represented by many peoples or nations. In either case the existential reality fails in large measure to conform. It remains excessively imperfect in terms of the perfect idea."

When you equate justice or righteousness with the people, you create a very evil social order. The people do not want justice or righteousness any more than criminals or capitalists, aliens, the middle classes, the lower classes, the upper classes, or any other class wants it. What they all want is their own will! This is why the modern state is in trouble. It embodies the will of man, a fallen will. True law must represent the righteousness of God and protect man from man, man from the state, man from himself. After all, our Lord said, "For out of the heart proceed evil thoughts, murders, blasphemies, adulteries, fornications, thefts, false witness." How can this heart create true justice or righteousness by saying, "Go to now, we will make us a law!"

God's law alone transcends men. God's law alone can give true justice, true righteousness, to men. Let me cite Dr. Howell once more: "Each community may be defined by its ruling idea. And the distinction between communities is their basic idea." Very true, except that Dr. Howell, not being a Christian, did not state this properly. Instead of "basic idea," he should have written their "basic faith." This is the identifying mark in any community, in any social order. Its faith is what governs its concept of law, of community, and of all other things.

Let us consider that a moment. If you believe in the Apostles' Creed as a summation of our Christian faith, what you affirm every time you say it is that you believe in the communion of saints. It is very interesting in this regard to go back to the pre-Norman Conquest church. At that time, when the English church repeated the Apostles' creed, they said that particular sentence in this way: "I believe in: of the saints, the society." What was recognized very clearly, and stressed by Archbishop Aelfric and others, was the fact that a social order is inescapably a society. Otherwise it falls apart and is at war with itself, beset by internal conflict. Instead of the people being members of one another, they hole up their houses, they do not care to know their neighbors, they are afraid of the people down the street, and they are afraid when they go into a strange neighborhood. There is no society.

Society is a religious fact. It is the culmination of our affirmation. When we say, "I believe in God the Father almighty and in Jesus Christ," and so on, we come finally to say, "I believe in: of the saints, the society," or, in modern English, "I believe in the communion of the saints."

The humanistic state cannot give community. The tragic fact is that all around us people seek communion today in sick and frenetic experiences, such as rock and roll. They feel a sense of community when they yield themselves to primitive and evil impulses. Or they feel that, fleetingly, they have a sense of communion in sexual experience. They seek communion and community in all kinds of experiences outside of God's righteousness, but it escapes them because it is an impossibility. There is no life and no communion, no community, outside of God. "I am the way, the truth and the life," Jesus said.

The Bible tells us that sin is any want of conformity unto or transgression of the law of God. The opposite of sin is obedience. Sin is disobedience. John says, "Sin is the transgression of the law of God." What is faithfulness? It is obedience to the law of God. If we separate justice from the law of God, we then have a humanistic definition of righteousness, and we attempt to build the Tower of Babel afresh. This is why God is bringing confusion on the world of our day. There is confusion from pole to pole. The end result of confusion will be death. There is no life, nor is there any justice or righteousness, apart from God and His law-word.

It is significant that the ancient world recognized that no state could exist apart from a doctrine of atonement. One of the amazing facts which we often forget when we approach history is that history is essentially religious, whether it is Christian or non-Christian. As a result, we have a dehydrated history in the textbooks.

Julius Caesar is an example. How did he triumph? Off and on for 300 years there had been a Civil War in Rome. It was between the old aristocracy and the plebeians, each working with equal savagery to gain control, and both very corrupt. Along came Julius Caesar to work against his own class and to gain power. He had a solution, he felt, expressed in one word — *clementia*. It meant forgiveness, the forgiveness of sins. As he won each battle and conquered part of Rome, people came to Caesar with all sorts of documented evidence of the corruption of the ruling order. In each instance, as they presented the data to him, he ordered a bonfire to be lit, and he said, "All is forgiven. The past is to be forgotten. There will be forgiveness of sins and we will create a new society."

Julius Caesar conquered Rome in terms of the forgiveness of sins; however, while Julius Caesar could say, "I forgive your sins," he could not change anyone's heart. The forgiven men were still unregenerate, as Caesar himself was. The very men whose offenses he forgave and whose corruption went up in a bonfire subsequently assassinated Caesar. They had not changed. But it was a religious program. The whole of the ancient world recognized — and they were ahead of us in this respect — that you can only build a social order on a religious foundation. That religious foundation, they said, was atonement. Thus it was that every year in Rome there were the annual rites of lustration, of atonement and cleansing.

Anyone who did not appear for the annual rites of atonement, unless he was a soldier in combat away from Rome, lost his citizenship. Businessmen had to make sure that their journeys were ended and they returned home in time, or they lost their citizenship. Rome held, as other cultures of antiquity did, that atonement was necessary, that guilty men were dangerous men, that men had to be transformed somehow or the social order would be destroyed. Of course, since their atonements were null and void, since they were unbiblical, their social orders were destroyed. They could not remedy the fact of sin, nor the fact that their laws represented the sin of man pretending to be righteousness. Each in turn fell.

The sad fact is that too often we have erred in the past centuries in saying, "Yes, the pagans were right. A foundation is necessary. It has to be the atonement of Jesus Christ." But, like Rome, we have tried to force it from the top down, which does not work.

No man can be saved by any edict of the state. If so, we would have a perfect world. The attempts to save society by compelling it to be Christian from the top down have been a disaster, whether by Catholics or by Protestants, and both have attempted it. Both, I believe, have learned better.

Our work is from the bottom up. It is to bring the power of God and His atonement to bear upon the life of every man, and thus to make it the basis of society. It is to make the law a part of our life, so that we represent God's righteousness in all of our being and in every area and sphere of life in which we are involved. Rome sought with all its might to effect righteousness in its own way from the top down, but it disintegrated.

The spirit of Rome was well-expressed. Paul refers to it in the aphorism, "Let us eat, drink, and be merry, for tomorrow we die." There is no meaning, no purpose to life except to get what you can while you can. That same Roman philosophy is prevalent today. It is interesting that, with this philosophy, the Romans also lost faith even in eating and drinking, and they could not be merry. That same aphorism is found in the ancient Egypt of Moses' day. They also concluded that eating and drinking gave no pleasure, that nothing gave pleasure, that life itself was a burden.

The most common inscription on the tombstones of pagan Romans was this: "I was not, I am not, I care not." It became so common that, for purposes of economy on many of the tombstones, it is not even written out in full. Just the initials for those words are given. It was expressive of the faith of Rome. Rome died long before it fell.

And the world around us is dying. It is dying because it does not know the righteousness of God unto salvation, because it does not know the atonement of Jesus Christ. It is dying because it refuses to apply the righteousness of God in its everyday life — individual, familial, church, societal, vocational and civil government. But it is urgently needed. This is why we are called to be the light of the world and to be the salt of the earth. Salt was a preservative. It was used to keep foods for times when you could not acquire them elsewhere.

The Indian reservation I ministered to was a long way from town. During the winter I was there, we were snowed in the Sunday before Christmas. It was not until mid-May that the Army was sent for to come in with its special equipment and dig out the road to the reservation. It was under sixty feet of snow. Naturally, in a winter like that, you cannot go across to the Trading Post and get food. They frequently run out, so you have to depend upon what you already have. During the summer I would catch all the trout I wanted because there were no limits on the reservation, and put it in salt brine so that it could be used later when there was nothing else available. The brine was the preserving agent.

The Lord says that this world, being fallen, is going to disintegrate into total anarchy, total chaos, apart from us. We are the preserving agency. We are the salt of the earth. Even as we preserve it from the total anarchy and decay which would overwhelm it on its own premises, we, as the light of the world, provide the light whereby the world is to be redeemed and made into the Kingdom of God. That is our calling.

We cannot hide our light under a bushel, or seek only to preserve ourselves in our own houses. Then we are only fit, our Lord says, to be trodden underfoot of men, again a practice which refers to the old use of salt. When spring came and we were through with the brine in which the meats were salted, we did not throw it out into the garden area because it would kill anything which might grow. We put it on the pathways where nothing *should* grow, where it was trodden underfoot of men.

Our Lord tells us that He reserves a particular judgment upon us — and judgment begins at the House of God — if we fail to meet our responsibility. To whom much is given, of him much shall be expected. The judgment that befalls Christians down through the centuries is a particularly severe one, because they have been so richly blessed and the blessings upon them are so great. We know what the curses of God upon faithlessness are to a covenant people, and what His blessings are. They are spelled out for us very plainly in Deuteronomy 28.

In every country where an oath of office is required, as is required in the United States by the Constitution, the oath has reference to swearing to almighty God to abide by His covenant, invoking the cursings and blessings of God for obedience and disobedience. We have a fearful responsibility, but also a glorious one, because all the promises of God to us in Christ Jesus, if we are faithful to our covenant calling, are "yea" and "amen." We are heirs in Christ of all things, in heaven and on earth. We are heirs of creation. We have a glorious calling.

Chapter Five

The Future of Justice

One of the great myths dominating the modern world is the concept of neutrality. Man is not, nor can he ever be, neutral. The human mind is not capable of neutrality, but always speaks from a particular perspective.

Similarly, man is not an autonomous creature. He is the creature of almighty God, totally dependent upon God and in all things subject to Him. We have today a false picture of reality. It is believed that man has an autonomous reason, that he is capable of neutrality, and that there is a realm of values which are somehow neutral and equally accessible to all men.

These concepts come from Greek philosophy. The Greek philosophers did not regard the good, the true, and the beautiful as coming from God. Rather, all values and all universals existed above and over God and man, and equally governed God and man. These Platonic ideas or forms or universals, which represented reason in all its purity, could be apprehended by the man of reason; therefore, the man of reason incarnated the universals in his own being and in the life of the state.

When the early church began its thinking, it was infected to a great degree by Hellenic thought. As a result, although the biblical doctrine of creationism militates against this neutral realm of values (which are separated from God, associated with reason, and therefore subject to incarnation in man), and although the early church rejected neutrality up to a point, because of its failure to appreciate the full significance of the doctrine of creation, the early church never broke with the great virus.

In this respect the rise of Darwinism was providential for the Christian church. It led to an attack on the doctrine of creationism and then to a defense of that doctrine, which has been especially notable since World War II. Because of the revival of creationism, we have seen a growing awareness of the implications of the fact that God is the Maker of all things in heaven and on earth, and that there can be no values and no universals which are detached from God and made to float somewhere in outer space.

As a result, we have seen a revival of Christian thinking to an unprecedented degree. We see it in the philosophical sphere, in the work of men like Dooyeweerd and Cornelius Van Til. We see it in the practical sphere in the Christian school movement, above all things, because, since all things are made by God and all things must be under Him, it follows logically that education must be under Christ.

Some would raise the question at this point of biblical law and its relationship to natural law. What is the relationship of natural law to these independent values? In the Greek context, natural law, such as they knew it, was the law of nations, where the nations were rational, and it was the law which was of value above and over God and man.

During the Middle Ages there were two facets of the doctrine of natural law. One of these, best expressed by Nicholas of Cusa in the Fifteenth Century, says: "Every decree is rooted in natural law. And if a decree contradict it, it cannot be valid. Whence, since natural law is naturally in the reason, every law is known to man in its root."

In a sense, what Nicholas of Cusa said was right. Scripture tells us that the heavens declare the glory of God and the firmament showeth His handiwork. Wherever we look, we see God's handiwork, His law, manifested in all things. But we must remember, whenever we look, that we look through eyes affected by the Fall. If we as redeemed men are still partially influenced by the Fall to a degree, because we are not perfectly sanctified in this life, how much more so the unredeemed. Saint Paul says in

Romans 1:18 that the natural man holds (or, better in Greek, "holds back, suppresses, sits down on, keeps under cover") the righteousness of God. All men indeed know God — the things visible and invisible of God. They know the law of God; it is written in every atom of their being. But they hold back or suppress this in unrighteousness, in injustice.

The other medieval perspective on natural law is found a century or so prior to Nicholas of Cusa, from Gratian, who said: "Mankind is ruled in two ways, namely, by natural law and by customs. The law of nature is that which is contained in the law and the gospels." Why is the Word of God the law of nature? Because the God of all creation gave it, and His Word is the law-word for every sphere. Therefore, according to Gratian and others of that school, we find in the canon, in the rule of Scripture, natural law. That law is over man, it is over nature, and it is over the nations. None can stand except in terms of that law.

The parable of the two foundations gives us a revealing insight into that fact, for our Lord said, "Everyone therefore that heareth these words of mine, and doeth them, shall be likened unto a wise man who built his house upon the rock." Note that in the Greek text, although not always in translations, it is "the" rock. The rock throughout Scripture is a symbol of the Lord. The only time it is not a symbol of the Lord, when it is used in a figurative sense, is when Moses declares of false religions, "Their rocks are not like unto our rock."

The parable is recorded: "And the rain descended, and the floods came, and the winds blew, and beat upon that house; and it fell not; for it was founded upon the rock. And everyone that heareth these words of mine, and doeth them not, shall be likened unto a foolish man, who built his house upon the sand: and the rain descended, and the floods came, and the winds blew and smote upon that house; and it fell: and great was the fall thereof." Just as the rock is Christ, so the sand is man. When we build the house of our social order, our personal lives, upon man, upon ourselves, we are as those who build upon sand. We must build upon the rock.

I said that there were certain prevailing myths which govern our age, one of which is the concept of neutrality, the belief in an independent sphere of values or universals separated from God. There is another myth which has ruled our age more than any other. It is very much a product of the modern world, and in particular of the philosopher Hegel: the belief in the conflict of interests.

If we believe in God, the God of Scripture, we must believe that there is an ultimate harmony of interests, that God made all things in terms of His sovereign purpose and that nothing can alter His triumph in His purpose. Everything in all creation works together for good. The most horrifying moment in all the history of mankind was when the Sanhedrin met secretly at night to plot the crucifixion of our Lord. At that moment, the most evil moment in history, John declares, "They did this that the Scripture might be fulfilled."

What a magnificent sentence! It tells us that man at his worst only furthers the plans of almighty God. The worst man can do still resounds to the glory of God. That is the doctrine of the harmony of interests. But what we have now is the doctrine of the universal conflict of interests: that all things work together for evil; that all life is a "dog-eat-dog" business, and that the only way to solve matters is to recognize the inevitability of conflict, and to make our methodology one of conflict.

One of our staff members, Otto J. Scott, wrote a book which was published by the New York Times Press. It began to sell phenomenally well until the New York Times Press found out what was in it. They immediately ordered that no more copies be sold and the entire edition be dumped. We managed to salvage it. The title of the book was *The Secret Six*, and it was about the life of John Brown, an American abolitionist. Contrary to what some books tell you, Brown was not a Christian prophet. He was a humanist. He was also a professional killer, hired by six very wealthy Unitarians to force a confrontation which would lead to war. Being Hegelians, they believed that conflict would lead to resolution, which would then lead to further conflict — perpetual war for perpetual peace.

John Brown instituted for us the politics of confrontation. Ever since then, throughout the Western world, we have had the politics of confrontation — demonstrations, riots, marches, evil — forcing issues, supposedly in order to resolve matters, but, in fact, only leading to the further aggravation of problems.

The conflict of interests is a very evil doctrine. We believe in the harmony of interests. When we fight the state on issues — and we are not afraid to fight — we believe we are working for the good of the state as well as the church. We believe that most sincerely. Mr. Ball is dedicated to Christian freedom, and he is also dedicated to the welfare of the American state, as are all of us in this battle. We believe we are fighting for both church and state, for their integrity and their development and the direction of Christian freedom.

Because we believe in an ultimate harmony of interests, we must say something which is very obvious to most, and yet, to some, appears not to be so: that there is no conflict in the Godhead. The Father, the Son, and the Spirit are not at war with one another. That sounds obvious enough, but apparently we have a great many people who, without saying so, are affirming that they are at war. If you declare that God's love and God's law are opposed to one another, or that love and justice are opposed to one another, or that mercy and wrath are opposed to one another, you are affirming that there is a conflict of interests in God, and I do not believe that. Not a single word of Scripture affirms that.

I appreciate the title of a book by an English writer dealing with the Puritans and their views on this matter — *The Grace of Law*. The Puritans rightly saw that law and grace could not be separated. I enjoy speaking on how the Doctrine of the Covenant tells us of this beauty and the unity of God's purposes for us. What modern theology has done is to sentimentalize doctrines and separate them. We talk about forgiveness as though it were an emotional matter. But forgiveness in Scripture is juridical. It means in its original meaning, "charges dropped because satisfaction has been rendered." It can also mean, "charges deferred for the time being." It is used once in this sense, when our Lord says from the cross, "Father, forgive them" — defer the charges for the time being — "for they know not what they do."

Moreover, love is not an emotional, antinomian, and lawless term. We are told very plainly in Romans 13 that love is the fulfilling of the law, and we are told this after the commandments are summed up: "Thou shalt not kill, steal, commit adultery, bear false witness, and if there be any other law, it is briefly comprehended in this — 'Thou shalt love thy neighbor as thyself.'"

What is the Scripture telling us? It is telling us that I do not love my neighbor simply because I get a little gushy and say, "I love you." I love my neighbor if I respect his right to life — I do not kill him, and I see that his life is extended the protection I want for mine. I respect the sanctity of his home — I do not commit adultery. I respect his property — I do not steal. I respect his reputation — I do not bear false witness. Nor do I covet — that is, seek by legal and/or fraudulent means to gain what is properly his. That is what it means to love thy neighbor.

Over the years I have had occasion more than once to talk to an adulterous husband or an adulterous wife who tells me, "Yes, I did it, but I love her," or "But I love him." They want somebody to say, "There, there. I know your heart was in the right place all the time." But I say, "No, you don't love that person. Don't tell me that. Love is the fulfilling of the law. When you commit adultery, you are expressing a hatred for God and for you spouse. If the word of God means anything, that's what it tells me. There is no dealing with your problem until you recognize that what you did was sin, and there was no love in it." Love is the fulfilling of the law. The word "fulfilling" does not mean ending or completion. It means putting into force.

With that in mind, let us look at the law again. When I speak about the law, the righteousness or justice of God, I must not say that the state is *the* ministry of justice, but *I* must be one also, as a redeemed man in Christ — a ministry of justice or righteousness. So too, my family, my church, my school, my calling, and my society. In every area we must manifest the righteousness of God, the law of God. If we do not, and if we leave justice to the state, we are in the same kind of trouble as if we leave Christianity to the pastor.

We dealt earlier with the Apostles' Creed and the fact that we make an affirmation of our beliefs in the communion of saints, "of the saints, the society." What does this mean? It means, says Paul, that we are members one of another. How do we show our righteousness one to another, as members one of another? It means we are mindful of the needs of the Body of Christ, and also of those outside the Body of Christ, because we are to do unto others as the Lord has done unto us. He has shown us His grace and mercy, and we are to be vessels of that grace and mercy and manifest it to others. This refers to a variety of activities which the

Christian must engage in, as an individual and as the member of a community.

One church in America, for example, has set up a very fine Loan Fund, to lend to a brother in need without interest, in terms of the plain commandment of Scripture. As the elderly and the young face problems which they cannot cope with financially, they can go to that Loan Fund and borrow. Thus far everyone has repaid their loans and added to the fund. The Trustees made it clear that, if their problems became insoluble, and at the end of six years they found they could not repay, the debt would be canceled. The requirement of the Lord is that we minister one to another, to the elderly and the sick.

The Christian school ministry is a remarkable one across the country, and the most dynamic area of growth at present in the United States is among the negroes. We are experiencing a major revival in the black communities. I mention the work of Dr. E.V. Hill in Watts, Los Angeles, where the rioting took place. Dr. Hill had dedicated himself to winning over to Christ all the ghettoes of the United States. There are seventy million people of all different colors in those ghettoes, and every revolutionary agency in the world is seeking to reach them. He says, "I know, because I was there as one of them." He was a modernist and a revolutionary. Years ago he was one of the younger associates of Martin Luther King, Jr. Now he is one of the finest preachers of the Gospel we have in the United States.

He has a congregation of five or six thousand, in the center of Watts, with members on every block, 31 blocks in every direction. He has a Christian school for hundreds of children. He is training every adult to reach every person on his block for Christ.

In one instance which delights me, the only person on a particular block was a blind black woman, and she was told, "Sister, let the Lord be your sight." She went from door to door with her cane and wound up with 161 out of 162 converted. The last one decided to move away — he was a young hoodlum, and he could not tolerate what was going on in his community. He refused to allow them to help him move. He was tired of all these "amen" and "praise the Lord" people. So, they found out from the truck driver where he was moving to, found that they had people on that block also, and called them. When he arrived there, his neighbors were ready to help him unload. After they were through, they told him, to his consternation, that they were doing it in the name of Jesus.

We have another pastor, a black pastor in the downtown area of Los Angeles. His name is Price, and he has a congregation of 15,000. He is buying the old campus of Pepperdine University and is going to make it a center to win for Christ all the people for miles around. He and his fellow ministers are reaching out and training everyone they can. This summer, I will be teaching a group of negroes who have started a church in the Oxnard area. They are beginning to do some remarkable things, and they want training in other things they can do to reach everyone in the area for Christ. Today that "black" church, with two black pastors, is about one-third Mexican, one-third white, and one-hundred percent on fire for the Lord. Of course, they are being troubled by the city officials. Everything is being done to frustrate them, because they are changing the character of the city. If they have their way, they are going to put the Welfare Department out of business and do it with grace.

Just before I left on a trip, I had a call from Margaret Jenkins. She is a black woman, not too young, who has started the Mary Celeste Christian School and is doing remarkable things there. It is having an increasing influence in that area, which was crime-ridden heretofore. She is bringing more law into that district than the police could ever maintain. So what have they done? She has a chain link fence around the property. The officials have ordered her to tear it down and put up a wrought iron fence which costs a dollar a foot. It would have cost her a fortune, because she has a sizable piece of property. This is the kind of harassment to which she is subjected. But it does not bother her. She says, "Those people at City Hall don't know. I serve a Lord who is greater than they are." She does not get discouraged.

This is how we conquer the world: a person at a time, as each sees the implications of the faith and becomes a living law; as each applies the very Word of God to his daily life and reaches out to others. Law, love, grace, mercy, judgment, are all aspects of God. We cannot pick and choose and say, "We are going to show the love of God, but not the law of God nor the justice of God." No, it is all one manifestation of the being of God, of His nature, of His plan for us, in and through our lives.

The result is that we are beginning to see some very dramatic things in the United States. The Press does not report them, but they are taking place, and they give us something for the future. When you look at the great buildings on city skylines, you do not see the buildings of tomorrow which are going to top those buildings. Right now they are just an excavation where the foundation is being laid. That is why the kind of thing which is going on all over the world today is not clearly visible. The Press is looking for the things which dominate the skyline, but that is the wave of the past.

In 1900 only three percent of Africa was Christian. When the African states gained their so-called Independence, it was eighteen percent and that was only twenty-five years ago! After Independence there was a wholesale massacre of Christians. In the Sudan area they were killed by the hundreds and hundreds of thousands. In Nigeria, the Ibo people finally sought to gain their independence, but the nations of the West conspired against the Ibos only to surrender them into the hands of the other peoples of Nigeria, and they were massacred in great numbers. In Uganda, we have a description from a native pastor of how the rivers in the past few years under Idi Amin have, at times, been choked with the bodies of Christians. Yet the church in Africa is now comprised of nearly forty-five percent of the population! Remarkable things are happening.

I recently had the privilege of talking with a French pastor, whom I have never met, although I had corresponded with him for some time. His father and mine, both pastors, had been friends in the Old Country well before World War I. Aaron Kayanan, now a leader in the French Reformed Churches, is in the United States, in Illinois, where he is taping daily broadcasts in French to France and Africa. "What is happening in Africa," he told me, "is unbelievable. We cannot begin to cope with the number of people who are becoming saved, are Christians, and are beginning to ask what they can do now to bring their lives totally under the Word of God. If we don't get busy, we are going to see them outnumber us and outperform us in Europe and the United States."

These people are not interested in Fire and Life Insurance, as too many people in church pews are. They are there for marching orders from the King of kings. This must be our concern, too.

The Christian School movement in the United States and in other countries is evidence that some people are beginning to hear those marching orders. The public school people are very much afraid of them. According to their own statements, if these schools continue to grow at the present rate, the public schools will, to all practical intent, have disappeared by the end of this century — only seventeen years away. One of them said to me, "Don't you realize! This will put us back into the Dark Ages, where everybody will be believing the Bible from cover to cover." I do not object to that. All we need to do is to put shoes on our faith and to walk with it.

Chapter Six

The Procession of Power

We tend, too often, to have a "box theology" approach to our faith. We treat theology and Christian faith as though it were a limited aspect of reality. As though the universe were the whole, and theology was restricted to a small corner. When we have a "box theology" perspective, we end up quarreling amongst ourselves, criticizing the Baptists and the Presbyterians and the Catholics and the Charismatics, or whoever else we disagree with, instead of setting forth the claims of God upon the whole area.

Our approach to doctrine is the same. We treat the doctrines of Scripture as though they had reference to things ecclesiastical. This is not the case. The doctrine of infallibility is an inescapable doctrine. I have written a little book called *Infallibility, an Inescapable Concept*, in which I point out that, if you deny the Word of God to be infallible, something else under the sun will proclaim infallibility, whether it is the state, the philosopher-kings, or some other human agency. You cannot deny the things of God without appropriating them for men.

We seem to think of justification as though it were purely an ecclesiastical doctrine, and yet we regularly say of people who are trying to excuse themselves, "He is trying to justify himself." Men require justification. If they do not get it from God through Jesus Christ, they will try to establish it for themselves. They pay a great

57

deal of money to a psychiatrist or a psychoanalyst to help them do it.

The same is true of atonement. It we deny the atonement of Jesus Christ, we will turn either to sadism (laying our sins upon another and punishing him), or masochism (punishing ourselves). All men outside of Christ's atonement will be sadomasochistic. They will seek atonement, alternating between sadism and masochism.

I submit to you that the foreign policy of the United States reveals something about the kind of atonement our humanistic United States seeks — a masochistic one. We punish ourselves endlessly. Conversely, the Soviet Union is sadistic. It lays its sin upon others: upon capitalism and democracy. You do not escape the force of biblical doctrine by denying the Lord. You simply transpose it.

My concern here is to deal with a key doctrine which I believe should be of very great concern in all of its implications, because again we have this problem of transposition. This is the doctrine of procession. It is spoken of throughout the Scriptures, but we have it set before us in one verse of Scripture as clearly as it can be set forth anywhere:

> But when the Comforter is come, whom I will send unto you from the Father, even the Spirit of truth which proceedeth from the Father, He shall testify of Me (John 15:26).

The Spirit in His procession comes as the Spirit of Truth in our hearts to give us the truth, to speak of the Father and to speak of the Son, to communicate power and knowledge to the believer. The procession of the Spirit is the communication of power. This is an inescapable concept.

In the 1920's, Kenneth Burke the liberal, humanistic editor of the *New Republic*, wrote a very interesting book, *Permanence and Change*, in which he spoke quite prophetically of that which he believed would come to pass before the century was too far gone. He said, very simply, that man needs power; man needs grace. We no longer believe in power and grace from above, and therefore man will seek them from below. And we will have a doctrine of power and grace from below of a demonic sort before the century is far gone. Indeed, we have seen the rise of occultism and men seeking the procession of power from below. And why not? In the thinking of the modern world, power does come from below. The universe has evolved, it is said, so that all that we see around us is a procession coming from the underground of creation. The power in the artist and the musician comes from the underground of the unconscious. This is the source of power, of creativity, of energy, and of a new kind of grace. The world believes very much in the doctrine of procession, but it seeks procession in the wrong area.

We have a process theology today, and process theology has captured many segments of the Church, both Protestant and Catholic. It is a perversion of the faith, to the doctrine of evolution, to a belief in the great chain of being rising out of the primeval chaos. As a result, we are returning to the cults of chaos which marked the ancient world. I wrote a little booklet about twenty years ago entitled, *The Religion of Revolution*, which analyzed the implications of the cults of chaos and their rise and return in the modern world.

One such cult of chaos familiar to us from the Greco-Roman world was the saturnalia. Morality was very strict in those days, but once a year, for a period of days — sometimes a week: in some cultures, ten tens — all law was subverted. A condemned man was brought out of prison and made the king, even to the extent of possessing the queen. Laws against bestiality, against incest, against any and every kind of perversion were subverted. Only one law remained, and that was that the bakers had to work long enough each day to produce food for the populace.

This came out of the Greco-Roman belief that all creation arose out of chaos, and therefore power, energy, and grace were present in chaos. In the annual release of chaos, that power was tapped and invoked, so that a procession out of the wellsprings of being would surge through society and give it vitality for another year.

Today in our music, in the sexual revolution, and in one thing after another, we see a resurgence of this: a doctrine of procession, but not of the Spirit. As a consequence of the revival of this kind of thinking, we have seen the rise of modern statism. The modern state does not derive its power from God. It derives its power from the world of nature, as the natural institution which sums up the will of the people. It is no longer the will of the nobility, or royalty, or aristocracy — not that we would agree with that either — but it has moved downward. Now minority groups are enthroned. Not because they need justice, but because the idea is that the lower they are, the closer they are to the wellsprings of power.

In the 1960s we had a great hue and cry about the negro being the downtrodden member of society. In *avant garde* circles today, the negro is out and the homosexual is in. The negro is no longer considered low enough socially to be regarded as the wellspring of vitality.

The doctrine of procession is thus basic to a social order. The doctrine of procession includes, not only the belief that power proceeds from a source, but also that processions accompany it — processions in the form of what we would call parades, rituals. Therefore, as the church triumphed, we had the procession of ecclesiastical dignitaries and staffs, of images and icons, of the host or the communion wafer, because the images or symbols of power were with the church.

As the state began to rise, we had a different kind of procession, the procession of the emperor. When the emperor entered a city he was hailed, "Blessed is he who cometh in the name of the Lord." This was the procession of power. However, although the emperor would proceed into a city with a certain amount of borrowed Christian terminology, he also proceeded with a parade of soldiers, indicating that, however much he might use ecclesiastical language, his power still rested on armament. So there began a different concept of the processional.

The university also began its processionals. We still have the academic procession today. The university claims to represent the true processional of being. We have, as a relic of that doctrine, the concept of academic freedom. The academician is not responsible to any human agency, because he somehow represents the voice of the wellsprings of power and is therefore beyond the touch of men. In other words, a rebellion has taken place in Christendom. Its roots go far back, deep into the medieval era. They began to surface with what we call the Renaissance. The Reformation and Counter-Reformation held them back for a time, but with the Enlightenment and supremely with the French Revolution, they came to the surface. Since the Russian Revolution they have been sweeping over the face of the earth. The belief is that the procession of power is from below, upward.

But God says that the procession of power is from the Throne of all eternity, unto us. We need today to reaffirm the doctrine of the procession of the Spirit. We need to manifest power and grace — the presence of the Spirit — to the world. God moves in this world to redeem men, and through men to reorder the societies and nations of this world and the institutions thereof.

We must deal with those things legally and theologically, which will enable us to manifest more clearly that procession of the Spirit, the procession of grace and power in our day, always recognizing that "greater is He that is in us than he that is in the world." We must see in the procession of the Spirit the marching orders for the conquest of all things. "Ye shall receive power, after that the Holy Ghost is come upon you, and ye shall be witnesses unto me; both in Jerusalem and in all Judea and in Samaria and unto the uttermost part of the earth."

It is the state's procession of power which is most apparent on the human landscape today. But it is increasingly a barren one, a failing one, because all it represents is naked power. There is neither a moral authority nor the righteousness of God. The more Rome asserted the deity of the emperor, the more barren its claims became, because the discrepancy between the claims and the reality of what was transpiring on the streets was so great. The emperor spoke about the glory of Rome, but in the last century or more, almost none of the emperors stayed in the city. It was not a safe place, even for an emperor and his troops. When Rome fell, the imperial court was at Ravenna. It has been at Milan and a number of other cities over the years. The glory had departed from Rome, because its moral authority was gone. It had only a procession of empty power left.

We are seeing something similar today, because the moral authority of the modern state is also declining, the more it departs from the Word of God. That moral authority can only be restored as the state sees the procession of power, not from below, but from above. We know that there is no procession of power to equal that which Christ promised, which Christ delivers, and which Christ commands us to claim.

According to the Word of Scripture, we are the people of His grace and of His power. This is why He could command His disciples and all of us, "All power, all authority, in heaven and in earth is given unto me. Go ye therefore and make disciples of all nations, teaching them all things that I have commanded unto you: and lo, I am with you always." The procession of power is always there, even unto the end of the world. Go ye therefore....

Epilogue

As noted in the Preface, these chapters are the edited transcripts of the addresses given by Dr. Rousas J. Rushdoony at the Logos Conference, "The Place of the Judeo-Christian Ethic in Today's Society."

In his summary at the conclusion of the conference, the Chairman, Howard Carter, referred to six primary needs which had come to light over the two-day period:

1. The need for a process of education on the relevant issues. He urged the delegates to take time to make themselves aware of the material available concerning the issues.

2. The necessity for the unity of interested parties — not doctrinally, but in the Holy Spirit. Mr. Carter said, "We cannot afford to speak against each other just because we do not agree with man's doctrine. We need to speak with one voice and with authority to Governments and to Education Departments. This is more effective as one voice than as fragmented groups."

3. The need for strategy. This is not a picnic. I cringe when I hear people say, "We are going to get into court and we are going to tell these guys what to do." Firstly, that is not Christian. Secondly, they are a lot more equipped in the battle than we are. There needs to be education, litigation, and legislation to win the battle.

4. The need to be aggressive rather than defensive. As the representatives of the King of kings, the church must not be put on the run. Write fearlessly to senators and parliamentarians and let our flag be shown. We have a mandate from God to salt the earth — light the world.

5. The necessity to support one another. If a pastor in your town goes to court, go along with him. Fill the court with a silent testimony of the Christian population. Stand with him and support him financially. Every victory won in court is a precedent we can build on in another court. Every step taken involves us all.

6. The necessity for prayer. Our confidence is in God, that the Maker of heaven and earth is in charge. Identify with movements committed to praying for the nation, for schools, for Christian parliamentarians and lawyers. No prayer which originates in heaven will be refused there.

The Author

Rousas John Rushdoony is a well-known American scholar, writer, and author of over thirty books. He holds B.A. and M.A. degrees from the University of California and received his theological training at the Pacific School of Religion. An ordained minister, he has been a missionary among Paiute and Shoshone Indians as well as pastor of two California churches. He is founder of Chalcedon Foundation, an educational organization devoted to research, publishing, and cogent communication of a distinctively Christian scholarship to the world at large. His writing in the *Chalcedon Report* and his numerous books have spawned a generation of believers active in reconstructing the world to the glory of Jesus Christ. He resides in Vallecito, California and is currently engaged in research, lecturing, and assisting others in developing programs to put the Christian Faith into action.

The Ministry of Chalcedon

CHALCEDON (kal•see•don) is a Christian educational organization devoted exclusively to research, publishing, and cogent communication of a distinctively Christian scholarship to the world at large. It makes available a variety of services and programs, all geared to the needs of interested ministers, scholars, and laymen who understand the propositions that Jesus Christ speaks to the mind as well as the heart, and that His claims extend beyond the narrow confines of the various institutional churches. We exist in order to support the efforts of all orthodox denominations and churches. Chalcedon derives its name from the great ecclesiastical Council of Chalcedon (A.D. 451), which produced the crucial Christological definition: "Therefore, following the holy Fathers, we all with one accord teach men to acknowledge one and the same Son, our Lord Jesus Christ, at once complete in Godhead and complete in manhood, truly God and truly man ...." This formula directly challenges every false claim of divinity by any human institution: state, church, cult, school, or human assembly. Christ alone is both God and man, the unique link between heaven and earth. All human power is therefore derivative: Christ alone can announce that "All power is given unto me in heaven and in earth" (Matthew 28:18). Historically, the Chalcedonian creed is therefore the foundation of Western liberty, for it sets limits on all authoritarian human institutions by acknowledging the validity of the claims of the One who is the source of true human freedom (Galatians 5:1).

The *Chalcedon Report* is published monthly and is sent to all who request it. All gifts to Chalcedon are tax deductible.

Chalcedon
Box 158
Vallecito, CA 95251 U.S.A.
www.chalcedon.edu